I LOVE TO HELP
أحبُ المساعدة

Shelley Admont
Illustrated by Sonal Goyal, Sumit Sakhuja

www.kidkiddos.com

support@kidkiddos.com

First edition, 2017
Translated from English by Hanan Ahmed
تُرجمها من الإنجليزية للعربية _حنان أحمد أبو شعرة
Arabic editing by Shahad Sam and Sara Shoshaa

Library and Archives Canada Cataloguing in Publication Data
I Love to Help (Arabic Bilingual Edition)/ Shelley Admont
ISBN: 978-1-5259-0433-2 paperback
ISBN: 978-1-5259-0434-9 hardcover
ISBN: 978-1-5259-0432-5 eBook

KidKiddos Books

For those I love the most

إهداء لأولئك الذين أحبهم

Jimmy bounced around the car in excitement.

لف جيمي حول السيارة في سعادة.

"We're going to the beach!" he shouted happily. "We're going to the beach!"

"إننا ذاهبون إلى الشاطئ!" قال بسرور. "إننا ذاهبون إلى الشاطئ!"

Dad laughed as he opened the trunk of the car. "That's right!" he said, "It's a lovely sunny day and we want to get going quickly."

ضحك الأب وهو يفتح صندوق السيارة وقال "هذا صحيح!"، "انه حقا يوم مشمس جميل وعلينا أن نتحرك بسرعة."

"Why don't you help us carry the things we need to the car? Your brothers are helping already."

"لم لا تساعدنا في حمل الأشياء التي نحتاجها للسيارة؟ ها هم إخوتك يساعدوننا."

Jimmy stopped bouncing and looked towards the front door of their house.

توقف جيمي عن القفز ونظر باتجاه الباب الأمامي لمنزلهم.

Jimmy's two brothers were helping carry things to the car.

كان أخوا جيمي يساعدان في حمل الأشياء إلى السيارة.

The oldest brother had colorful buckets and spades in his hands, and the middle brother was carrying the picnic basket.

كان الأخ الأكبر يحمل في يده دلاء ومجارف ملونة، بينما يحمل الأخ الأوسط سلة للنزهة.

"Come, Jimmy!" Mom called from the doorway. "You can carry the bag of towels or this small beach chair. It won't be very hard."

نادت الأم من مدخل الباب "تعال يا جيمي!"

"يمكنك حمل حقيبة المناشف أو كرسي الشاطئ الصغير هذا. لن يكون الأمر صعباً عليك."

Jimmy looked at the towels and chair. "No, thank you!" he said with a grin. "I'm too busy JUMPING!"

نظر جيمي إلى المناشف والكرسي وقال مبتسماً "لا، شكراً! أنا أقفز ومشغول جداً!"

The forest where they lived was not too far from the beach and Jimmy wriggled with excitement the whole way.

لم تكن الغابة التي يعيشون فيها تبعد كثيراً عن الشاطئ وأخذ جيمي يتحرك من الحماس والسعادة طوال الطريق.

When he saw the golden sands of the beach and the sparkling blue water of the sea, he started jumping in his seat.

وعندما رأى رمال الشاطئ الذهبية والمياه الزرقاء المتلألئة بالبحر، بدأ يقفز في مقعده.

"Alright, we are here," said Dad.

"حسنا، لقد وصلنا" قال الأب.

Jimmy got out of the car. "This is amazing," he exclaimed and ran down towards the water.

خرج جيمي من السيارة. وصاح "هذا رائع!" وركض نحو البحر.

"Wait!" Mom called after him. "You've got to help us to take everything out of the car."

نادت عليه أمه "انتظر! عليك أن تساعدنا في إخراج كل شيء من السيارة."

Jimmy turned around, waving at his family. "No, thank you!" he said. "I've got to build a GIANT SANDCASTLE!"

استدار جيمي ملوحا بيده لأسرته وقال "لا، شكراً! سأذهب لبناء قلعة عملاقة من الرمال!"

He ran to a perfect spot on the beach, right next to the sea, and started to scoop sand into his hands.

جرى إلى مكان مثالي على الشاطئ، وبدأ يغرف الرمل بيديه.

Jimmy was so busy having fun that he didn't notice his family going to and from the car, carrying objects down to the beach.

كان جيمي مشغولاً للغاية لدرجة أنه لم يلحظ عائلته وهي تذهب وتأتي من السيارة، تحمل الأشياء وتضعها على الشاطئ.

Meanwhile, the sandcastle grew bigger and bigger

وفي هذا الوقت، كبرت القلعة الرملية أكثر وأكثر.

"My castle is going to be so big, a King and Queen are going to want to move in!" Jimmy said, imagining tiny knights and servants running around inside.

قال جيمي "ستصبح قلعتي كبيرة جدا وسيود ملك وملكة في الانتقال إليها!" قال ذلك متخيلا فرسان وخدم صغيري الحجم يركضون في الداخل.

While Jimmy was working on his castle, his older brothers were hunting for shells.

وبينما كان جيمي يبني قلعته، كان أخواه يجمعان الأصداف.

Dad went swimming in the sea and Mom lay on a towel further up the beach.

وذهب الأب للسباحة في البحر بينما تمددت الأم على منشفة على الشاطئ.

Jimmy was so focused on his castle that he didn't really notice what the rest of his family were doing until...

وكان جيمي منشغلاً بقلعته لدرجة أنه لم يلاحظ ما تفعله بقية العائلة حتى......

"Watch out!" Jimmy heard his dad shout.

"انتبه!" سمع جيمي أباهُ ينادي.

He looked up just in time to see a giant wave rising up beside him from the sea!

والتفت ليجد موجة عملاقة آتيةً من البحر ترتفعُ بجانبه!

"Oh no!" cried Jimmy as the wave crashed down on top of him. When the water pulled away, Jimmy lay on his back and tried to catch his breat

صرخ جيمي "أوه، لا!" و ارتطمت الموجة به. وعندما تراجعت المياه، كان جيمي راقداً على ظهره يحاول أن يلتقط أنفاسه.

"Yuck!" Jimmy spat out salty water and pulled seaweed from behind his ears.

أووع!" بصق جيمي الماءَ المالح وسحب الأعشاب البحرية من وراء أذنيه."

Then he looked up to see
what had happened to his castle.

ثم التفت ليرى ماذا حدث لقلعته.

"Noooo!" he cried. The castle was completely destroyed!

وصرخ "لاااااااااا!" لقد تحطمت القلعة بأكملها.

Jimmy felt hot tears on his face as he looked at the ruined castle.

نزلت دموع جيمي بحرارة على وجهه وهو ينظر إلى القلعة المدمرة.

Mom knelt down beside him and gave him a hug. All his family had stopped what they were doing and gathered around him.

انحنت الأم بجانبه واحتضنته. وتوقفت عائلته كلها عما كانوا يفعلون وتجمعوا حوله.

"I'm sorry about your castle," Dad said.

قال الأب، "أنا آسف بشأن قلعتك."

"Yeah, your castle looked really nice," said the oldest brother.

وقال الأخ الأكبر "نعم، لقد كانت قلعتك تبدو جميلةً حقاً."

"And big," agreed the middle brother.

وقال الأخ الأوسط متفقا معه "وكبيرة."

Mom smiled. "Don't worry, Jimmy. We'll help you build a new one."

ابتسمت الأم وقالت "لاتقلق يا جيمي. سنساعدك على بناء واحدة جديدة."

"You will?" Jimmy asked.

تساءل جيمي "أحقاً ستفعلون؟"

"Yes!" His family laughed and they all set about building the sandcastle again.

"أجل!" ضحكت عائلته و بدأوا في بناء القلعة الرملية مرة أخرى.

Something was different this time. Jimmy realized that with his family helping him, the castle was bigger and more beautiful than before.

شيءٌ ما كان غريبا هذه المرة. لقد أدرك جيمي أنه عندما ساعدته أسرته، كانت القلعة أكبر وأجمل من ذي قبل.

"Look!" the oldest brother pointed inside. Two crabs had settled down in the center of the castle. "It even has a King and Queen!"

أشار الأخ الأكبر إلى داخل القلعة وقال "انظرا!". لقد استقر اثنان من سرطانات البحر بداخل القلعة. "لقد أصبح أيضا بالقلعة ملكٌ وملكة!"

Jimmy bounced up and down. "This is the best sandcastle ever!"

قفز جيمي فرحاً . "إنها أفضل قلعة رملية على الإطلاق!"

When it was time to go, the family began taking things back into the car.

وعندما حان وقت العودة، بدأت الأسرة تأخذ الأشياء وتعيدها للسيارة.

Jimmy grinned. "May I help you?" he asked.

ابتسم جيمي وسألهم "هل يمكنني مساعدتكم؟"

He took the towels to the car and then ran back to help carry the buckets.

أخذ المناشف للسيارة وجرى راجعاً ليحمل الدلاء.

"Wow, we packed that really quickly," Dad said when they were done, looking at the empty beach.

قال الأب عندما انتهوا وهو ينظر للشاطئ "رائع، لقد جمعنا الأشياء بسرعة حقا."

Even when they came home, Jimmy continued to help, carrying the beach chairs back into the house.

وحتى عندما رجعوا للمنزل، استمر جيمي في المساعدة، وحمل كراسي الشاطئ وأعادها للمنزل.

"Everything works out better when we help each other," he told Mom.

وقال لأمه" كل شيء يعمل بشكل أفضل عندما نساعد بعضنا البعض."

Mom smiled. "Well, the car is empty now, except for one thing."

ابتسمت الأم وقالت "حسنا، السيارة خالية الآن فيما عدا من شيء واحد."

Mom pulled out a packet of cookies. "I think someone needs to help eat these cookies!"

سحبت الأم علبة بسكويت. "أعتقد أن شخصا ما يحتاج للمساعدة في تناول البسكويت!"

Jimmy laughed.
"Yes, please! I'll help."

ضحك جيمي "نعم، من فضلك!
سأساعدك."

CPSIA information can be obtained
at www.ICGtesting.com
Printed in the USA
LVHW07*1708060918
589366LV00029B/549/P